Community Helpers

Construction Workers

by Cari Meister

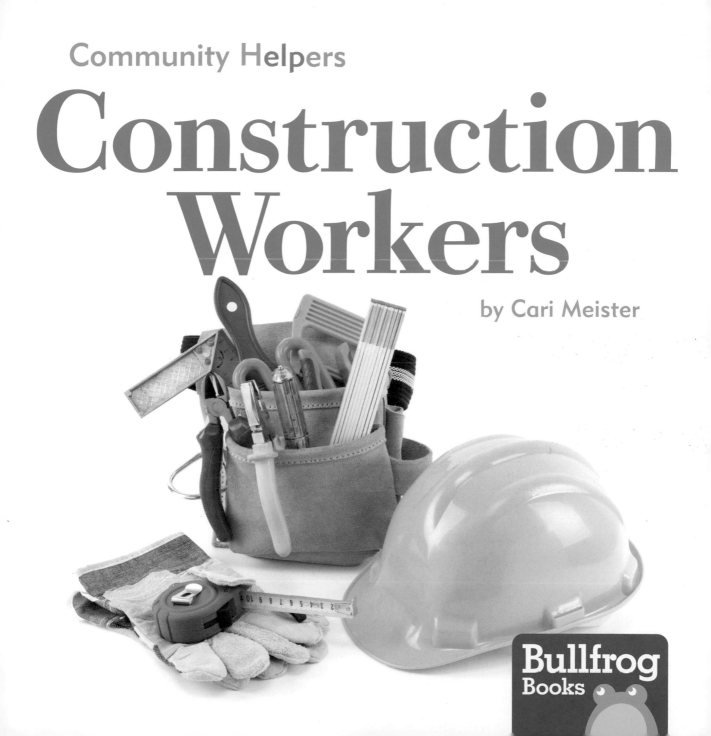

Bullfrog Books

Ideas for Parents and Teachers

Bullfrog Books let children practice reading informational text at the earliest reading levels. Repetition, familiar words, and photo labels support early readers.

Before Reading

- Discuss the cover photo. What does it tell them?

- Look at the picture glossary together. Read and discuss the words.

Read the Book

- "Walk" through the book and look at the photos. Let the child ask questions. Point out the photo labels.

- Read the book to the child, or have him or her read independently.

After Reading

- Prompt the child to think more. Ask: Where have you seen a construction worker? Have you seen him or her building something? What was being built?

Bullfrog Books are published by Jump!
5357 Penn Avenue South
Minneapolis, MN 55419
www.jumplibrary.com

Library of Congress Cataloging-in-Publication Data
Meister, Cari, author.
  Construction workers / by Cari Meister.
    pages cm.— (Community helpers)
  Summary: "This photo-illustrated book for early readers explains what construction workers do and how they work to build things in our community."— Provided by publisher.
  Audience: 5-8.
  Audience: K to grade 3.
  Includes index.
  ISBN 978-1-62031-090-8 (hardcover)
  ISBN 978-1-62496-158-8 (ebook)
  ISBN 978-1-62031-134-9 (paperback)
  1. Building—Vocational guidance—Juvenile literature.
  2. Construction workers—Juvenile literature. I. Title.
  TH159.M45 2015
  690.092--dc23
                          2013037885

Editor: Wendy Dieker
Series Designer: Ellen Huber
Book Designer: Lindaanne Donohoe
Photo Researcher: Kurtis Kinneman

Photo Credits: All photos by Shutterstock except Alamy 16-17, 17, 23tr; Corbis 10-11; iStock 10, 20, 22, 23 br; Superstock 21

Printed in the United States of America at Corporate Graphics, North Mankato, Minnesota.
6-2014
10 9 8 7 6 5 4 3 2 1

Table of Contents

Hard at Work

Leo wants to be a construction worker.

What do they do?

They read plans.

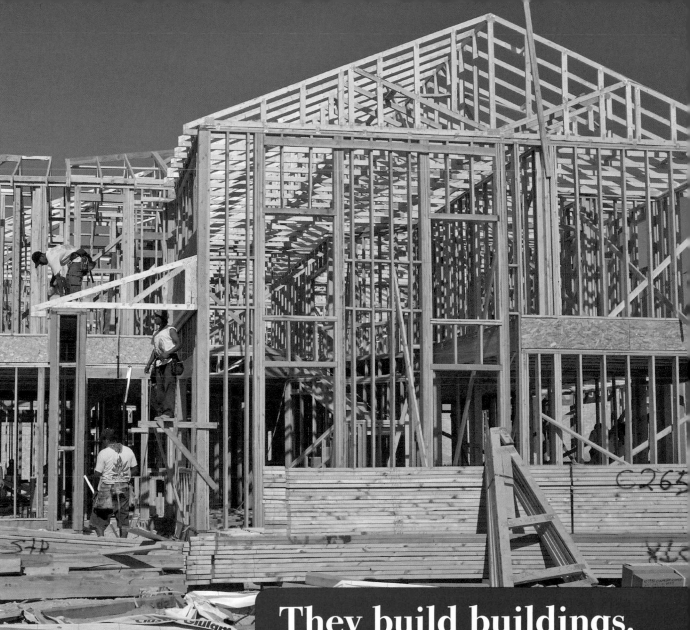

They build buildings.

A school is falling apart.

It is old.

It needs to be torn down.

Max works the crane.

It has a wrecking ball.

Smash!

It crashes into the wall.

wrecking ball

Ty has a jackhammer.
The bit goes up and
down very fast.

It breaks up old cement.

bit ....▸

13

What a mess!
A crew cleans up.

Time to build!

Roy pours cement.

It goes into a frame.

When it dries, it will be
a hard wall.

frame

Bam. Bam.

Kurt has a nail gun.

He makes a roof.

nail gun

What a lot of work!
Now the school is done.

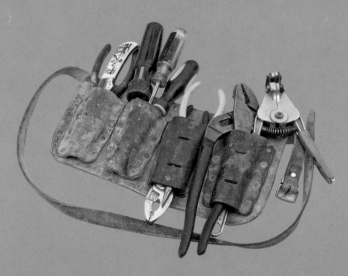

On the Job Site

hard hat
Workers wear a hard hat to protect them from falling things.

tape measure
A ruler that rolls up.

tool belt
Workers keep tools handy on a belt.

foundation
The base of a building. It might be made of cement.

Picture Glossary

bit
A piece on the end of a drilling or hammering tool.

frame
A structure that makes a shape; cement is poured into a frame until it dries.

cement
A mix of clay, limestone, and water that hardens when it dries.

plans
Drawings of what a building will look like when it is done, also called blueprints.

crew
A group of construction workers doing the same job.

wrecking ball
A heavy metal ball that swings from a crane, used for destroying buildings.

Index

To Learn More

Learning more is as easy as 1, 2, 3.

1) Go to www.factsurfer.com

2) Enter "construction workers" into the search box.

3) Click the "Surf" button to see a list of websites.

With factsurfer.com, finding more information is just a click away.